STRANGE OF OLD EDINBURGH

By Ian Ansdell
Illustrated by John Mackay

LANG SYNE
Publishers

STRANGE TALES OF OLD EDINBURGH was first published by Lang Syne Publishers Ltd, Old School, Blanefield, Glasgow G63 9HX in 1975 and printed by Waterside Printers at the same address.
Reprinted 1977, 1979, 1981, 1983, 1985, 1987 and 1989.
Copyright Ian Ansdell 1975
ISBN 0946264 53 8

INTRODUCTION

It is fascinating to think that a single development can change the character of a city. Today's Edinburgh has a reputation for being staid and aloof, but things were different a couple of centuries ago. Laird and commoner lived in close proximity in the closes and luckenbooths of the Old Town. The crowded tenements promoted a seemingly irrepressible vitality, and as Scotland's capital, Edinburgh provided the stage for centuries of political and religious drama. Much of this richness of life was lost, however, when Craig's plans for a classical New Town were put into effect. The broad, austere Georgian streets and their spacious houses seemed to sap the city's energy. The nobility had already moved to London or withdrawn to their country estates following Union with England in 1707, and now the middle class lawyers and merchants packed their bags and crossed the new North Bridge to form a genteel society that has left an indelible mark on Edinburgh's way of life.

We should mourn the passing of those earlier times, but not without giving thought to the darker side of life in the old days. There was dreadful poverty and overcrowding, for example, and no amount of the love of life can combat disease born of poor sanitation and poorer diets. And the years of war and insurrection took their toll of the citizens' finer feelings - human life was all too often held as cheap, and the pages of Edinburgh's history are liberally sprinkled with blood shed through callousness and brutality.

Finally there was religion. The Reformation ushered in an age of great religious uncertainty, and heresy and non-conformism of any shade were met with pitiless crudity. Much of the fuel for this fervour was provided by the deep-rooted superstition of the time. Walking through the city's dark and narrow wynds, with the houses towering starkly above, it must have been difficult not to feel a chill as one remembered the tales of ghosts and witches that circulated so freely in those precarious days.

Most of the stories in this book are drawn from this vibrant period in Edinburgh's past. Not all of them have their origins in the centre of the town. The fears and passions engendered in the High Street were equally real to the people of Warriston, Corstorphine, Morningside or Broughton, which were then villages outwith the city boundary.

We have chosen to illustrate some events by linking them with present-day equivalents of the taverns that played such an important part in fuelling the conviviality and effervescence of old Edinburgh. There are also a few more modern tales, and an interlude devoted to the curious belief that the capital was the scene of even more colourful events than those the history books already describe. We wish you pleasant reading.

THE COVER ILLUSTRATIONS:
Grim secrets of the Wrychtishousis — see story "Death at Bruntsfield".

A terrified 'witch' flees the flames

WITCHCRAFT

The Witches of Broughton

The persecution of witches was carried out with appalling ferocity during 250 years of Scottish history. No less than 17,000 people - mostly women - were tortured and executed between 1479 and 1722.

The methods used to extract confessions from suspects were barbaric. Burning with hot irons, pressing of thumbs and legs in vices, and forcing victims to wear iron boots which were alternately heated and cooled were among the least of the harrowing ordeals inflicted by the pious inquisitors of the Church.

It was a cruel and credulous age - innocent people could be strangled and burned on the word of someone who had a grudge against them. King James VI himself took perverse pleasure in attending the trials - he wrote a textbook on the subject, and once asked an unfortunate woman to produce a strom as proof of her powers!

But the Barony of Broughton - now part of Edinburgh - was notorious even in those hard times for its treatment of offenders. Where Barony Street now stands there used to be an ancient 'Witches Howff' - a narrow and sinister house, said to be used by a coven. Women believed to be members of the coven were among the victims of the Barony's frequent mass burnings. In 1608 the Earl of Mar protested to the Scottish Privy Council that some poor wretches had been burned alive, "after such a cruel manner that some of them died in despair, renouncing and blaspheming God". Others, covered with flames, managed to escape, only to be thrown back onto the fire until they died.

There is little doubt that some people did believe they had supernatural powers, or were in contact with the Devil. But the suffering needlessly meted out to blameless citizens is a terrifying blot on Scotland's history.

Agnes Finnie

In 1644 Agnes Finnie was charged with the most serious crime one could commit in those turbulent days, except treason - murder by witchcraft!

A small boy had run past her house in Potterow, calling names at her as he went, and Agnes - furious at his childish insults - told him he'd go lame. Sure enough, a few days later the boy was dying in agony from a paralysis that had started in his leg.

A torrent of accusations from neighbours followed her arrest. Beatrix Nisbet claimed she's lost the use of her tongue. The head of the city's shoe-making guild had suddenly faced financial ruin after a dispute with Agnes' son-in-law - his fortunes improved when he and the old woman settled their differences.

And worst of all, it was said that she had caused the death of another neighbour, Jonet Grinton. He had bought some haddock for Agnes at her request. They turned out to be rotten, and she asked for her money back. He refused, so she swore he'd never eat again in this world - within a fortnight Grinton had died of a disease that stopped him eating.

As far as the investigators were concerned, the evidence was overwhelming. Agnes Finnie was accused of having consorted with Satan for twenty-eight years, and of being notorious as a "rank witch". She confessed - after who knows what awful tortures - and was burned at the stake.

Coffins on Arthur's Seat

Five Edinburgh lads found more than they bargained for when they went hunting rabbits on Arthur's Seat one summer afternoon in 1836.

A dog they'd taken with them started scratching at the hillside. One of the boys went to investigate and found what looked like the entrance to a tiny cave.

He put his head inside to see what was there, and quickly withdrew it again. The hole was full of coffins!

There were seventeen of them, arranged in three tiers. Each one was four inches long and carved out of single pieces of wood, apart from the lids, which were fixed on with brass pins. The sides were decorated with minute tin designs.

The boys - unaware of the stir their find was to cause - immediately broke some of the coffins by throwing them at each other. But next day they gave the rest to their schoolmaster, who belonged to the local archaelogical society.

Curious, he prised the lid off one of them, and was amazed to find a diminutive figure inside, carved in perfect detail. Further inspection showed that the other boxes had the same bizzare contents.

Soon Edinburgh was buzzing with the news of the boy's find. There were endless discussions about the origin of the coffins, and even the London 'Times' devoted half a column to the story.

Could it be that the macabre miniatures were designed to bring about the end of some witch's enemy? It is possible, but to this day the coffins - some of them are now in the National Museum of Antiquities in Queen Street - have kept the strange secret of their origin.

One of the boys found what looked like the entrance to a tiny cave

The schoolmaster prised the lid off one of the tiny coffins

Angelical Thomas

Edinburgh's most infamous pair of Satanic malefactors were never actually convicted of witchcraft, yet their activities became firmly impressed on the minds of the city's ordinary folk as being connected with the Devil.

They were Major Thomas Weir and his sister Jean. Born in Carluke in 1599, Weir received his rank after active service in Ireland with Montrose's Covenanters. On his return to civilian life he became a captain in Edinburgh's City Guard, and it's said that he commanded the guard when Montrose was executed in 1650.

Weir remained a strict Covenanter, so he took up residence in the now demolished West Bow, which linked the Lawnmarket to the Grassmarket. There lived several members of a sect that suited his beliefs - the "Bowhead Saints".

They were a sanctimonious lot, who spent most of their time either praying or congratulating themselves and each other on their piety. They held meetings in their names, and Weir became so important in the group that he was able to choose where he would pray. Only the houses of "Saints of the highest Form" were good enough for the Major.

He was certainly an impressive character. He was tall, and dark in complexion, and a contemporary writer tells of his "grim countenance". To complete the effect, he usually wore a dark cloak, and carried round with him a tall black staff, carved with the heads of fabulous creatures.

The women of the group called him "Angelical Thomas", so imposing was his appearance, and so fine his praying voice. The members asked for his advice on problems, and coveted his presence at meetings.

Weir continued in this happy situation until 1670, and then events took a turn that none of his flock could have anticipated in their wildest nightmares. Their cosy world was shattered when Thomas revealed that he had been leading a double life. The front he had presented to them for twenty-five years, reflecting all that they aspired to, was a sham.

It was a dramatic moment. The cream of the Bowhead Saints were in the Major's house, expecting to listen to him pray. Instead, they heard a minutely detailed catalogue of a lifetime of fornication, bestiality, and incest with his sister.

The congregation were appalled. They concluded that Weir must have taken leave of his senses, and concluded that he must be made a prisoner in his own home before his confessions became public and brought the whole group into disrepute.

Word was passed around that he was dangerously ill, and the cover-up worked well enough for a few months. But the shallowness of their religious zeal was to be their undoing.

The Reverend John Sinclair, a minister at Ormiston, was among those who heard Weir's story. He had always been envious of the Major's preaching ability, and decided to discredit him by telling the whole story to the Lord Provost, Sir Andrew Ramsay.

Ramsay's reaction was the same as the Saints'. He arranged for Weir to be examined by doctors to find if he was sane. They reported that he was - his only problem, they said, was a ravaged conscience. When clergymen made the same diagnosis, the Provost had no alternative but to order Weir and his sister in the Tollbooth.

If James was sane, it seems that the same could not be said for his sister. Though the charge against her was incest, she proceeded to shock her examiners with endless tales of communion with the Devil. She revealed the mark of a horse-shoe on her brow, and told how she and her brother had travelled to Musselburgh in a flaming coach to make an undertaking with Satan.

She explained that the Major's staff was an instrument of magical power. It was the source of the skills that the West Port sect had found so irresistible, and allowed him to live his twilight life without discovery - for as long as his nerve held, at any rate.

Weir corroborated her story, and on 9 April, 1670, the pair appeared in the Justiciary Court, Charges of sorcery formed the bulk of the indictments faced by Jean, but her brother was mostly accused of debauchery of various sorts.

Surprisingly, considering the age in which they lived, they were acquitted on the charges of witchcraft. It was rare in those days for the magistrates to pass up the chance of doing away with anyone who professed the vaguest connection with the 'Muckle Deil'.

But they were found guilty on the other charges, and sentenced to death. 'Angelical Thomas' met his end at the Gallow Lee, an execution site near where the Playhouse Cinema now stands. He declined to make a final prayer for forgiveness. "Let me alone," he said. "I have lived as a beast, and I must die as a beast." He was duly strangled and burned at the stake.

Jean's last act as she stood before a huge crowd on the Grassmarket gallows was to try to remove her clothes! The executioner managed to salvage what little dignity there was in the situation, and she was hanged.

Predictably, the West Bow house that had once been a haven of godliness came to be regarded as haunted by spirits of a less holy kind. The Major's magic staff was reported to open the gateway to Hell, letting in strange spirits which danced till dawn. Weir himself was seen, galloping down the narrow streets on a fiery, headless horse. And occasionally passers-by reported seeing him arrive at his former home in the Devil's coach, drawn by six black chargers. The meetings of the Bowhead Saints were never quite the same again!

Major Weir and his headless horse!

CITY OF GHOSTS

Death at Bruntsfield

One of the grimmest of Auld Reekie's ghost tales concerns the Wrychtishousis, an ancient mansion that stood at the edge of Bruntsfield Links on the site now occupied by James Gillespie's School.

In the middle of the 18th century it was occupied by General Robertson of Lawers, who was staying in Edinburgh while his Perthshire home underwent alterations.

On the first morning of his stay the General was amazed to find his servant in a state of abject terror. The man claimed he had been visited by ghosts—a headless woman had been pacing the floor, he said, carrying a young child.

Robertson abruptly dismissed the servant's story, and refused to let him move to another room. But the spectral visitations persisted, and by the time the household moved back to Perthshire the man was thin with worry, and in a poor state of health.

The incident was forgotten until some years after the General's death, when his niece received a visit from a friend at Lowes. The Wrychtishousis had been the home of this woman's family, and in the course of conversation she asked if anything strange had happened during Robertson's stay.

The servant was quickly summoned, and was only too glad to tell of his terrible experiences. A grim story then unfolded which gave awful substance to his tale.

Renovations to the house had revealed a hidden closet. Horrified workmen found in it a chest containing the skeletons of a woman and a baby. And worst of all, the box was too short to hold the woman's outstretched body—so her head had been cut off and laid by her corpse.

A confession written by the perpetrator of the deed was also found in the closet.

Many years before, the Wrychtishousis' owner had gone abroad to war, leaving his wife and child in the care of a younger brother. But the man died in battle—and the brother murdered his widow and son to gain ownership of the house.

One wonders if the servant would have slept any better at Bruntsfield if he'd known about the awful secret hidden in the wall near his bed!

In the Wizard's Lair

Not all of Edinburgh's spectres were as terrifying as the one that appeared in the Wrychtishousis.

Early last century a soldier named William Patullo moved with his wife into the house in the West Bow where Weir the Wizard had spent his infamous life. The house had been boarded up since the Wizard's execution at the stake in 1670.

No-one had dared even to enter the place for fear of a dreadful fate, and the neighbourhood was alive with speculation about the terrors in store for Patullo.

Sure enough, as he and his wife lay in bed on their first night in the place, a wraith appeared—in the form of a calf! It stood at the end of the bed, then put its fore-feet on the mattress and gazed unblinking at them for sometime before it vanished.

Their experience was a great disappointment to the gossips, who had expected more sensational events. But it was enough for the Patullos. They found quieter accommodation, and the Wizard's lair was once more closed up.

Morningside's Green Lady

It was a happy day for Sir Thomas Elphinstone when he visited his life-long friend, the Earl of Glencairn, in London. For he fell in love with the Earl's daughter, Betty, who was forty years his junior.
Sir Thomas asked Glencairn for the girl's hand in marriage, and immediately received his friend's permission. But Betty was less than happy about the situation. She was in love with a dashing young officer, whom she knew by his regimental name of Captain Jack Courage.

Unfortunately, Jack had been posted to Ireland, and so the wedding went ahead. Elphinstone and his bride moved into his mansion, which still stands in Morningside, overlooking Craiglockhart and the Myreside playing fields. Now only one thing remained to make Sir Thomas' happiness complete - that Betty should meet his son, John, who was serving in the army.

Four months after the marriage John came home, and Betty discovered to her horror that her new step-son was none other than her lost love, Jack Courage. The situation was for him to leave the house. It was a sad and tender moment when the young couple said their farewells a few days later.

John begged a first and last kiss, and they embraced, only to be interrupted by Elphinstone coming into the room. As soon as he realised what was happening, the old man flew into an uncontrollable rage, and stabbed Betty through the heart with a dagger.

Immediately he broke into tears, and begged his son's forgiveness. John lifted the corpse, and laid it on the bed upstairs. The next morning, he returned to the room, to find his father kneeling beside the bed with his arms around his victim. He was dead.

They were buried together, but Betty's body was more easily laid to rest than her soul. John leased the mansion, and his tenants were horrified to see Betty appear before them, wearing the green dress in which she had died.

An oriental mystic was called in to communicate with her. She complained that her coffin was too close to Elphinstone's. A new vault was built, and some years later Jack Courage's coffin was placed beside that of his lover. The Green Lady was never seen again.

The Grange Inferno

For our next story we travel to Gilmerton, where a similar tale of thwarted love unfolded many years ago.

In 1320 Sir John Herring was at the height of his power. Laird of Gilmerton and Liberton, he was famous for his raids over the Border into English territory. He had a problem, however, in the form of his daughter Margaret, a beautiful girl, but moody by nature.

Melancholy and prone to fits of depression, she became a devout churchgoer, and almost every day she trekked three miles over the rough countryside to Newbattle Abbey. There she received religious instruction from one of the monks.

But her teacher was young and handsome, and soon their relationship strayed into less virtuous territory. They became lovers, and arranged to meet at the Grange, a small farmhouse in Gilmerton.

At first their secret was safe - the Grange was owned by a young widow who was also having an affair with a monk from Newbattle. Gossip soon caught up with them, however, and one night Margaret came home to find Sir John in a terrible rage.

He ordered her never to see the monk or go to the Grange again, but despite his wrath, she decided to visit here lover once more to warn him about the situation. It was a fatal mistake. The Laird discovered that she was missing, and set out over the fields with some of his men to the farmhouse. The door was locked, and he called to his daughter, but her fear kept her silent.

Sir John was incensed, and in his fury he grabbed a torch from one of his servants, and set fire to the house. The enormity of what he had done hit him as soon as the flames started to rise, but by then it was too late. He could only stand and listen to the screams of his daughter, the widow, and their lovers as they died a horrible death in the inferno. Immediately the Laird, stricken by grief and remorse, fled to France. His lands were confiscated by the king. But no earthly monarch rules the path where spirits walk, and locals say that Margaret's ghost still returns to the scene of her death. She last appeared in 1960 - 650 years after she perished.

White Lady of Corstorpine

Walking along Dovecote Road in genteel Corstorphine, one would hardly expect to be confronted by the spectre of a White Lady, pacing her ghostly path in eternal torment. Nevertheless, several people have reported seeing her.

The innocent sycamore in one of the resident's gardens, and the circular, three-storey building that gives the street its name, testify to a grim and passionate scene that was enacted there nearly 400 years ago.

Christian Nimmo, wife of a prosperous Edinburgh merchant, was in love with James, Laird of Forrester. The sycamore was their meeting-place, and they spent many happy hours together there.

Horror of the Grange Inferno

Christian Nimmo kills her husband

Now she wanders through eternity as a ghost

Terror death in the Haunted Attic

But Lord James had his faults - he was continually in debt, and spent too much time in the local taverns. One night, when he was the worse for drink, they quarrelled and he insulted Christian viciously. She brooded on his churlishness for a few days, then rushed to see him at his home, Corstorphine Castle.

It turned out that he was drinking again, so Christian sent her maid to fetch him from the Black Bull in the High Street. James was in a furious temper when he arrived at the sycamore. Instead of apologising, he renewed his attacks on her, and in her anger she pulled his sword from its scabbard and killed him.

Horrified by what she had done, Christian dashed to the Castle to hide, leaving her lover in a pool of blood. But she was soon found. There could be no doubt about the verdict at her trial, and she was sentenced to death.

She managed to have the execution delayed twice, and even escaped from the Tollbooth prison where she was imprisoned. But on 12 November, 1679, Christian Nimmo finally paid the price for her passionate deed, and was beheaded.

It is said that she can still be seen wandering near the sycamore, dressed in white and carrying a bloodied sword. Moreover, an awful curse hangs over the Dovecote - if it's demolished, says the legend, the lady of the house in whose grounds it stands will die within the year.

The Haunted Attic

About a century ago a street of tall, dark houses occupied a site now filled by new flats, near the Botanical Gardens. Neighbours were full of gossip about a man who lived in one of them. Good looking and well-to-do, he rarely left his home, and never received visitors.

Eventually he died. The house was locked up, and lay vacant for many years. Residents on either side claimed they could hear strange voices coming from it, but they soon stopped, and most people forgot about them.

Then, at the beginning of the First World War, an Englishman took over the property, and opened it as a boarding house. Its peeling paint-work was renewed, and the rooms were let - except the attic, from which voices were heard once more.

One day, when business was going particularly well, and all the other rooms were full, the landlord rented the garret to a young couple. They, too, heard someone talking inside, and rang for the house-keeper. The unfortunate woman opened the door and walked in, then let out a piercing scream.

The couple found her standing by a bed, gazing upwards. She was speechless with terror, and remained so for the rest of her life. There was a presence in that attic more dreadful than her sanity could cope with!

The story reached the University, and a Divinity student named Andrew Muir decided to find out for himself what was happening. He arranged with the landlord to go into the room with two bells. He would ring one if he saw something, and the other if he needed help.

He entered the attic at ten o'clock one evening. A few moments later the landlord heard both bells ring, and dashed into the room. Andrew Muir was sitting at a table, with a look of inexpressible horror on his face. He had died instantaneously of sheer terror. The house was locked up again, and the awful room never saw the light of day again, until the demolisher's hammer erased its secret for ever.

THE NEW JERUSALEM

Edinburgh has had many descriptions applied to it in its long and turbulent history, but surely the strangest is the claim that Scotland's capital and the biblical Jerusalem are one and the same place!

The claim is made in "Britain, the Key to World History", written some thirty years ago by Comyns Beaumont, a journalist. Israel's Jerusalem, he says, in no way corresponds to descriptions of the city which appear in the Bible or in the works of Josephus, the Jewish historian of Roman times.

But according to Beaumont the geography of Edinburgh tallies exactly with the old accounts of the Holy City. Edinburgh Castle fits the biblical description of Zion, the Citadel, and the Castle moat evidently solves a problem which has puzzled scholars for years. According to II Samuel, "David dwelt in the fort, and called it the City of David. And David built round about from Millo onwards". Experts have never conclusively worked out what or where Millo was in Jerusalem. But Beaumont is confident that it's the moat, which protected the Castle from attack from the Esplanade.

The Esplanade itself corresponds to Mount Opel and the Upper City of Jerusalem, while at the head of the High Street, the Lawnmarket marks the site of Upper Market Place. The ravine now partly filled in and spanned by George IV Bridge is the Tyropoean Valley of biblical times, which was dominated by the great Tower of Antonia, built by Herod to guard the Temple. Hadrian ordered the tower to be razed, and Beaumont claims that the great heaps of debris which formed the foundations for Edinburgh's Mound—linking Princes Street to the High Street—were the long-forgotten remains of the Antonia.

Next come Bezetha and the Pool of Bethesda. Bezetha was a 'new town', built across the Valley of Jehoshaphat and the Pool of Bethesda from the Holy City to accommodate the overflow from Jerusalem's expanding population. Beaumont points to the foot of the Calton Hill and the site of Princes Street as Bezetha. Between them and the Old Town lie the valley now occupied by Waverley Station and Princes Street Gardens—all that remains of the Nor'Loch, drained when Edinburgh's New Town was built.

Not all of Beaumont's 'proofs' are in the city centre. He suggests that Arthur's Seat—the extinct volcano that looms to the south-east of Princes Street—is in the exact position where the Mount of Olives should be. And Holyrood House, which sits at its base, corresponds to King Solomon's cedar palace, the House of the Forest of Lebanon.

The author sees Joppa as easy justification for his theory. Jerusalem's port has that name, and Edinburgh, too, has its Joppa by the sea, now largely swallowed by Portobello. Beaumont concludes his case by identifying Corstorphine Hill with the biblical Mount Tophet—the Place of Burning—and the Gogar district with Golgotha. The Place of Skulls where Christ was crucified is not in Israel, he claims, but four miles from the centre of Edinburgh.

Beaumont claims that there was a vast conspiracy to place the scene of old Israel's history thousands of miles from where they actually happened. The only thing that's certain about the affair is that Auld Reekie's citizens would be only too grateful for a conspiracy to replace their dreich winter days with Jerusalem's heatwaves!

CRIMES OF PASSION

Robert Weir

Murder at midnight put a brutal end to the life of John Kincaid, Laird of Warriston, one July night in 1600. It was four years before his killer came to justice, but his wife, who had engineered the crime, was brought to book more quickly.

Lady Warriston - born Jean Livingston, daughter of the Laird of Dunipace - harboured a passionate loathing of her husband. No record of her trial has survived, so the cause of her hatred died with her. Rumour has it that Kincaid was a brutal man. Theirs may have been a marriage of convenience between two influential families. On the other hand, Jean may have been in love with someone else, for she gave birth to a child shortly before the murder, and according to a contemporary ballad the Laird claimed it was not his.

Whatever the reason, Lady Warriston contacted Robert Weir, one of her father's servants, and told him that she could not bear to live with her husband any longer. Weir agreed to help her and on the evening of July 1 she hid him in a cellar in Warriston house. At twelve o'clock he crept upstairs to Kincaid's room and, with Jean watching, struck him a heavy blow.

It if had been effective, the plot might never have been discovered. But Weir had been clumsy - the Laird woke up and started to fight back. They struggled for some time, as Weir tried to throttle his victim, and Kincaid screamed for help. But soon the master of the

The Laird of Warriston attacked as his wife looks on

house was dead, and Lady Warriston sat in the hall in a state of shock, horrified at what she had done.

Weir fled the city, promising Jean that if the murder was discovered he would not betray her. It was a noble gesture, but unnecessary. The truth came out quickly, and the Magistrates were just as swift to order her execution. She was hanged within a few days, and in June, 1604, Robert Weir paid a terrible price for his part in the crime. The idea of a servant killing a laird was outrageous, and he was sentenced to be broken on the wheel.

Jessie King

In March 1889 Jessie King the 'Cheyne Street Baby Farmer', achieved the doubtful distinction of being the last woman to be hanged in Edinburgh. Her trial two months earlier aroused much disquiet in the city, not only because of the callousness of her crimes, but because of the circumstances that encouraged them.

King was charged with 'adopting' three babies from their mothers for £3 each — and then strangling them. There was no doubt about what the jury's verdict would be. The case had come to light after a bundle containing the body of a child was found in Cheyne Street. Statements from residents led the police to King's house, and there in a coal-closet they discovered the corpse of another child.

Further inquiries suggested that another baby had met a similar fate at King's former home in Dalkeith Road, but charges were dropped because the body could not be found.

King — described by an eye-witness as "mean, furtive, shabbily sinister, like a cornered rat" — was sentenced to death. She left behind her a world of grim poverty and straight-laced morals.

Jessie had obtained one of her victims through an advertisement for adoption in a newspaper, and was one of thirty who replied to it — a circumstance which prompted much comment at the time.

She tried to place another of the babies in an orphanage, but was refused—because it was illegitimate. And as a final irony, her landlady testified that one day King had gone out to give birth to a child of her own—and returned without it. Was it, too, 'adopted'?

Cheyne Street now houses a new Day Centre for old people—testifying to a more enlightened age than the one that sealed Jessie King's fate.

Nicol Muschat

September 5, 1719, was an unlucky day for Margaret Hall. It was the date of her marriage to Nicol Muschat - outwardly a promising young medical man, but in fact a callous good-for-nothing who was to send his bride to her grave just over a year later.

Muschet, learned early in life the pleasures available in Edinburgh at the turn of the century. Nevertheless, he trained as a medical student, and after a brief apprenticeship to a surgeon in Alloa he returned to the capital to work as an apothecary's assistant.

Then he met Margaret. Muschet claimed later that pressure from his friends and the girl forced him into marriage. Whatever the reason, they were wed - but only two months later he was planning to leave his estate in the hands of an administrator and desert her.

The plan fell through after complications and Nicol had to find another way out. Then he met James Campbell of Burnbank - whom he described in his confessions as "the only Vice-regent of the Devil". But he was happy enough to act on Campbell's suggestions for getting rid of Margaret.

He paid a friend of Burnbank £50 to lure her into a compromising situation, so that a fraudulent divorce could be obtained. When this failed, he embarked on a fantastic series of bids to murder the girl. First he tried poisoning her with mercury. She spent weeks in agony, but recovered. Then he hired footpads to kill her in a close. Despite several attempts - which Margaret evaded by sheer luck - this ploy also failed.

Eventually Muschet decided to do the deed himself. It seems incredible that she still harboured any love or trust for her husband. But she offered no objection when he asked her to go to Duddingston with him through the King's Park late at night on 17 October, 1720.

At the last moment she realised what he intended, but it was too late. He murdered her, and left her lying on Duke's Walk. But his last attempt was as clumsy as the others, for he left a sleeve at the scene of the crime. Muschet ended his miserable life at the end of the hangman's rope.

Eugene Chantrelle

A similar case to that of Nicol Muschet happened over a century later. The victim this time was Elizabeth Dyer, who at the age of fifteen, fell in love with her french teacher at Newington Academy. Eugene Chantrelle was certainly a romantic figure. Born in Nantes in 1834, he was a distinguished student at the city's medical school, and looked forward to a successful career. His father died when the boy was fifteen, however, and he had to leave school to support himself.

From then on Chantrelle became a drifter, unable to fulfill his early potential. He fled France for political reasons, and lived in America for some time. Then, after four years in England, he came to teach in Edinburgh. A handsome charmer with an air of cynicism, it is understandable that the young girl found him attractive.

Unfortunately, Eugene responded to her infatuation. Within a few months she became pregnant, and at sixteen she was married to Chantrelle in order to save her reputation. Before long, she was to pay for her good name with her life.

The evil Nicol Muschat is about to strike . . .

Chantrelle knocks over the table in a rage

They moved into a house at 81 George Street, and almost immediately Chantrelle's anger at the situation in which he found himself began to show. He beat Elizabeth continually, and spent as much time as he could away from home in the city's taverns. In 1876 he appeared in court, charged with assaulting a servant and threatening his wife.

Elizabeth's position became increasingly desperate, but she refused to leave for fear that publicity in the divorce court might harm her three children. But by 1877 Chantrelle had given up teaching, and was in considerable debt. That October, he insured Elizabeth's life for £1000 against accidental death.

On New Year's Day, of the next year, she became ill, and shortly afterwards she died in the Royal Infirmary. Chantrelle claimed that a gas leak had killed her. But the police had their own ideas about the cause of Elizabeth's death.

A doctor diagnosed narcotic poisoning, and traces of opium were found on the girl's nightdress. A quantity of the drug was found in Chantrelle's room, and his gas story collapsed when a long disused pipe was found. It had been deliberately fractured.

Chantrelle was found guilty of murder after a four day trial, and hanged.

William Bennison

Religious hypocrisy was never far beneath the surface of Edinburgh life, but the case of William Bennison is one of the worst of false piety.

Born in Ireland, he married an Irish girl, Mary Mullen, in 1838. Soon afterwards he left her, and bigamously married Jean Hamilton, of Paisley. Then he returned to Mary, and asked her to come to Scotland with him. When they arrived, she died mysteriously, and was buried in an unmarked grave.

He went back to Jean, and they moved into a house near Leith Walk. They had a daughter, and lived happily enough for several years. Both had strong religious convictions, and they became enthusiastic and hard-working Methodists.

But Bennison's attendance at prayer meetings took a distinctly unspiritual turn. He began to see a girl called Margaret Robertson, and soon afterwards told friends that his wife was in bad health. In fact she was perfectly well - but not for long. In February 1850 he bought some arsenic from an apothecary, and within a fortnight Jean was painfully ill. The ghoulish Bennison declared to her sister when asked for a doctor; "it is no use, she is going home to glory.".

He took a pair of black trousers to be mended, saying he would need them if his wife died, and later the same day she did. Bennison peomptly took the wedding ring from her finger, and moved in with Margaret Robertson's family.

But his sister-in-law was suspicious, first when he refused to allow a post-mortem, and then when a neighbour's dog died after eating the remains of the food he had used to poison Jean.

There was nothing the police could use as evidence, however, but the murderer's arrogance betrayed him in the end. He went to the apothecary from whom he had bought the arsenic, admitted he had used it to kill his wife, and asked the incredulous chemist to do him a service by not mentioning it to anyone!

Justice soon caught up with William Bennison, and he was hanged. But not before he had stood in the dock and called on Heaven to forgive the Crown witnesses!

William Sinclair

Student sit-ins are often thought of as an unfortunate symptom of our times, but few people know that they hold a time-honoured place in Edinburgh tradition!

One of the main centres of such activity was the Royal High School. "Barring out" of masters took place several times during the late 16th century, usually in support of claims for an extra holiday.

The pupils would gather a store of food and arms, then lock the school doors. Usually the buildings had to be taken by storm, and then there were fines to be paid and painful punishments to be received. Occasionally boys were jailed, and sometimes holidays were reduced instead of extended.

On 15 September, 1595, there was another "barring out", the start of an affair that would eventually involve the King himself. The school's quaintly-named Rector, Hercules Rollock, was first to arrive on the scene.

He was met by barricades, and a demand for a holiday. He reasoned with the boys, then threatened them, but they would not budge. Eventually he gave up, and asked the Magistrates to help.

Soon a group of city officers arrived, led by Baillie John McMorane. He also tried to persuade the boys to leave. When they refused, he ordered his men to break down the door with a battering ram.

The pupils shouted dreadful threats as the door began to give way. The Baillie would receive "a pair of bullets through his head", according to one boy. Sure enough, a few moments later one of the ring-leaders, William Sinclair, aimed a pistol through a window, and shot McMorane in the head.

His men were dumbfounded, but soon Sinclair and seven of his colleagues were in the Tollbooth. The Town Council convened, and sent a message to King James VI.

James decided that since the boys belonged to noble and powerful families, it would be against his interests for any action to be taken against them. They went to trial, but were acquitted on James' orders - because they were all under fourteen years of age!

Royal High School pupils riot!

TAVERNS

Greyfriars Bobby
Candlemaker Row

This pub commemorates one of Edinburgh's best-known stories—of a dog that stayed faithful to its master for fourteen years after his death.

Bobby, a Skye terrier, belonged to a Pentlands shepherd named John Grey. At the end of his working life, Grey—better known as Auld Jock—came to Edinburgh. There he died one winter night in 1858, in a dark, cold garret in the Cowgate, and Bobby's long vigil began. From then until 1872 he kept watch day and night beside Jock's grave in Greyfriars' Churchyard.

Bobby ate at Traill's Dining Rooms, near the cemetery, where the old shepherd had lunched on market days. In 1867 John Traill was taken to court for owning an unlicensed dog—as Bobby's story came out, the Lord Provost declared that he would be responsible for the Skye.

From then on Bobby's fame knew no bounds. Queen Victoria enquired after his health on visits to Balmoral, and when he died in 1872, and was buried beside his master, a Baroness paid for a memorial to be erected to his memory.

Bobby's memorial still stands opposite the pub that bears his name. There are two bars in this fine old tavern and in the stone-floored passage between them a colourful plaque tells the dog's story.

Prestonfield House
Priestfield Road

Prestonfield is a spacious and elegant mansion near Duddingston Loch, with at least its fair share of odd tales.

Built in 1687 by Sir James Dick, then Provost of Edinburgh, it replaced a house burned down six years earlier by students, who were protesting because some of their colleagues had been jailed by Sir James for burning an effigy of the Pope.

The Provost seems to have had an unusually morbid nature. He spent almost £2,000 on his wife's funeral, most of it on drink to keep guests happy while he regaled them with long passages of dreary verse dedicated to his dear departed.

Dick anticipated his own funeral by ordering a coffin several years before his death. Unfortunately, it was made of lead and weighed half a ton, and so wide that when efforts were made to take it upstairs it crashed through the staircase. Undaunted, Sir James kept flowers in it until he died.

His grandson, Alexander, chose a less dramatic road to fame. He made a fine medical reputation for himself—based on rhubarb! He was among the first to cultivate the plant and recognise its pharmaceutical value, and Dr Johnson was one of many who visited Prestonfield to sample the new delicacy.

The mansion was the scene of grimmer happenings in 1830, when it was rented by the Dowager Lady Gifford. Her two daughters looked out of the window one morning and saw a ghostly coal-black coach drawn by black horses and laden with passengers in deep mourning. No-one else saw the apparition, but fortunately it does not seem to have been an ill-omen for the girls.

Prestonfield is now a hotel, with a fine restaurant and bar which stand witness to the House's fascinating history.

Deacon Brodie's

Lawnmarket

Deacon William Brodie was one of the 18th century Edinburgh's most celebrated characters. A city councillor, he had a thriving wrighting and cabinet-making business.

The Deacon's social life was always full—a whirl of gambling, dice-playing and long hours spent in the Old Town's many taverns. But his greatest love was betting on cockfights—as popular then as horse-racing is today.

Even the £10,000 fortune he had inherited was not enough to finance his recklessness, and so he turned to crime, using his knowledge of Edinburgh society and business to carry out a series of minutely planned burglaries.

No-one suspected Brodie's secret life until one of his accomplices betrayed him after a raid on the city's Excise Offices. As soon as he realised he had been found out, the Deacon fled to London and took ship to Holland, where he waited for a boat to New York.

But on the way he made the fatal mistake of giving a fellow-passenger some letters to deliver in Edinburgh. The authorities were told, and Brodie was soon found and brought to trial.

On 1 October 1788, a crowd of 40,000 came to see the Deacon hang—on a gibbet he had designed himself. Twice he mounted the gallows, and twice the gibbet refused to work.

But the third time there was no mistake, and Edinburgh's most notorious councillor was dead.

'Deacon Brodie's Tavern' is a large establishment, well endowed with panelling and momentoes of the burgling Burgess. There's a stained-glass window on the stairs to the upstairs bar.

Blue Blanket

Canongate

Scotland was in an unruly state in 1481. The young king James III was at peace with the English, but his own barons were far from loyal. Eventually they would slay him at Stirling, but for now they were content to imprison him at Edinburgh Castle.

James appealed to Edward IV of England for help, and the Duke of Gloucester was sent to Edinburgh with ten thousand men. They were joined on the Borough-moor by a large company from the city, ready to rescue their King.

A bloodless solution to the affair was reached, and James was freed. The next year, in gratitude for their loyalty, he granted the craftsman of Edinburgh a banner, as well as certain rights and privileges.

The heraldic designs on the banner were embroidered by Queen Margaret herself, and it became a rallying-point for the citizens in time of war or civil disturbance.

The craftsmen were so proud of the Blanket that elaborate tales were later made up to give it on even more worthy origin than it already had.. According to one writer, the Order of the Blue Blanket was begun by Pope Urban II in about 1200 - making it the oldest order in Europe.

He went on to claim that it was carried at the head of a large contingent of Edinburgh folk on their way to the Crusades.
It's a good story, and unfortunately untrue. But the fact remains that even now every citizen - not only of Edinburgh, but of Scotland - is still technically bound to rally round the Blue Blanket if ever it is unfurled to help the Sovereign's cause.

The 'Blue Blanket' pub is fairly new, but stands on the spot where the city's old trade guilds used to meet. It's a comfortable bar, and good lunches are served.

Burke and Hare
High Riggs

There were sinister goings-on in Edinburgh in 1828. The University's medical research was famed throughout Europe, and attracted a growing number of students, but it depended on a rare commodity—corpses!

The anatomists needed bodies to teach dissection to their students, so they were prepared to pay as much as £14 for one. And no questions were asked about where the cadavers came from—a point which was not lost on William Burke and William Hare, a pair of Irish labourers.

Between February and October of the year, Burke and Hare provided the surgeons with 16 bodies. All had met the same fate—lured into Hare's cheap boarding house in the West Port, they were plied with whisky until senseless and then smothered.

The murderers had a narrow escape in April, when a medical student recognised the corpse of a young girl, but their grim trade was only ended when visitors found one of their victims and called the police.

Hare avoided punishment by turning King's Evidence and betraying his accomplice. Burke was hanged in the Lawnmarket on 29 January 1829—and his body taken to the School of Anatomy for dissection!